# Whore Moans

## (A Hoetry Book)

by

## Chris Sheerin

A book by

darkWolf press

darkWolf press, 5 Orlan House,
20 Strand Road, Derry BT48 7AB
Tel: 07597691377
Email: darkwolf62@rocketmail.com

1 - hormone *n. (physiol.)* Substance secreted by a ductless gland or formed in an organ (as insulin in the pancreas, or sex hormones in the testis and ovary) and carried by the blood stream to a specific organ which it stimulates.

2 - Whore moans (descriptive) The sexual grunts and growls of a bed-hopper who, having made the beast with two backs, is intent upon having her fumbling bed mate feel as if he is the biggest man she has engaged in *coitus* with that evening.

3 - Whore moans *collective noun* (pun, descriptive) A term applied by disgruntled males to a wanton female who, though blessed with more worldly gifts and goods than a Walmart depot on Black Friday, constantly bemoans her lack to every male within earshot.

# Not So Blue Hoetry

# Until Death

We pledge to take on the secret you:
> The dark fiend we pray never to see.
> She who skulks in your inner cellar;
> She who's all we dread she may be.

Yet we cannot possibly contain her,
> For she's a mistress of deepest night.
> And as she lays in bed, overthinking,
> We can sense that we're in for a fight.

She'll recall each wrong that befell her:
> Every slight, both imagined and real.
> And she'll realise we need reminded
> That she got the raw end of the deal.

There is only one way to subdue her:
> Apologise, hug her fast, kiss her head;
> Say you'll love her forever, and cuddle;
> Turn around and pretend you are dead.

# You Read Porn

You detest me for reading porn,
>Yet you read Fifty Shades of Grey.
>And because I ogle other women,
>You're convinced I'll be led astray.

And yet when you devour erotica,
>It's without even a hint of shame:
>So, you're envisioning men naked,
>But I'm the one getting the blame!

Besides, women say sex is cerebral,
>Claiming it and love are the same.
>So, aren't you effectively cheating,
>As I play the world's oldest game?

# Hormones

You'll never be rational,
 You'll never be reasonable;
 Every one of your thoughts
 Will forever be seasonable.

You see, logic is a process –
 One that's fairly consistent:

Yet, hormones swiftly express,
 Before the owner, in distress
 – and feeling under duress –
 Begins to obsess and reassess;
 After which, she'll regress,
 And regretfully acquiesce,
 Before frankly claiming that
 – totally crushed by stress –
 She became a possessed mess,
 Thusly keeping reason distant.

# Aftermath

The tongue is a Sword that never Rusts:
      And so, woe betide He Who Entrusts
      His deepest secrets to She Who Talks.

You'll regret the day you break her trust:
      She'll use your private info to implicate,
      Incriminate, complicate and insinuate,
      Until whispers are squeaks and squawks.

She'll spice titbits up to improve flavour:
      Intentionally doing so to curry favour
      With all your friends, before she walks.

# Ever Wrong?

You admitted you weren't right:
> You'd been somewhat unkind,
> And wanted to make amends.

You said it was your monthly:
> Your hormones; women's things.
> But, if we could put it behind us,
> We could probably stay friends.

Now, we're back, going strong:
> And, everything is great, except
> You've *never* said you're wrong!

You expect it from me, though:
> You need a penitent admission,
> Then a heart-rending contrition,
> Plus flowers, dates and rings.

So, are you ever fucking sorry?
> And no, it's not about semantics:
> Yours is a perpetual power-play,
> And that's just one of your antics!

# Woman's Wrongs

The Japanese have it right:
    She walks two steps behind.
    The Muslims have a point:
    Burkas keep her confined.

Ethiopians: A hole in the lip;
    This stops her from drinking.
    Vanuatu: Cranial deformation;
    Stops her from overthinking.

Aborigine: Ring through nose;
    This stops her from straying.
    Europeans: Too many rights;
    No playing until we're paying.

# Reignite

We attempted
  To reignite
  An old flame:
  But, by using
  Used matches,
  It was more
  Of the same

We were charred,
  Fire-scarred,
  Burnt to a crisp,
  Will-o-the-wisp.

You are to blame:
  You're all gas –
  Mouth and ass.
  So, a fire-starter
  Only in name.

# Lebensraum

I have enough clothes, I do,
    Yet there's something I covet:
    I need more storage space,
    In the wardrobe and the closet.

Ever since you moved back in,
    I feel very much out of place:
    Like Germany annexing Poland,
    You've reclaimed Living Space.

You're basically a Jackboot Jill,
    And appear to hold the power.
    But what if that's just the start?
    I'm afraid to fucking shower!

# Cry Baby

Look, it used to work:
    A single tear, here or there.
    But then I woke up to it all:
    All of that fake despair.

You would be envied by:
    A – professional mourners;
    B – snared wild animals;
    C – manic depressives;
    D – extra-strong diuretics;
    E – juicing machines;
    F – drama obsessives.

You have cried me a river:
    So, now I'm going sailing,
    As I'm sick of being the Wall
    At which you keep Wailing!

# Housework

As for cooking and cleaning,
     They're in no way demeaning,
     If performed by the lesser sex.

You're studying housewifery,
     And you're a domestic scientist.
     So ask: What can I analyse next?

You were born just for this:
     Because why else are you here?
     And you know this is the case.

So, grab a handful of dusters,
     Stop answering us back,
     And, woman, know your place!

# Palimony

Palimony: So,
    You'd like me
    To openly attest
    To just give you
    It all afterwards,
    Then *still* be
    Your friend?

Alimony: Isn't
    It more honest?
    We can re-enact
    How we loved:
    Fighting over
    The petty stuff
    Until the bitter
    Fucking end!

# Trust Issues

I hate when we have to talk:
>     You call them 'must' issues.
>     And yet, when you add, 'Now!'
>     I know you mean trust issues.

In short: You can't trust me,
>     But need to know you can.
>     In short: The real reason is
>     I'm simply a fucking man!

You can't trust me for an hour.
>     But, what is trust? Let's define:
>     It's hanging about nine months
>     To see if it's fucking even mine!

# View

You can see right through me:
    Well, that's according to you.
    Yet you keep on coming back,
    So you clearly enjoy the view!


# Faker

You, girl, are faking it –
    But I'm faking it, too.

You fake your orgasms:
    But I can go one better,
    For I fake it every time
    That I say I love you.

# Sleeping Late

You are freezing cold, every single night,
    Yet you are 1000 degrees every morning.

So, I wake, tired as hell, and start yawning,
    Trying to convince myself to just get to it,
    Yet you drape a lazy arm around me.

Helpless, I acquiesce without any fight,
    As you drag me gently back into our lair:
    Soothing me with your radiating warmth,
    Suggestively purring you need me there,
    That I should delegate and let others do it.

Only to later complain that nothing's done,
    And delegate the blame to the guilty one.

# Pale Blue Hoetry

# Angry Cat

When I'm doing you hard from behind,
  You're not supposed to arch that way:
  The ass is *always* higher than the back,
  So your best bits are forever on display.

Didn't they teach this in sex education?
  Hard fact: Sex has nothing to do with you.
  You are simply showing off your wares:
  Would sir like Trap One or Trap Two?

So, just lie there and open your twat,
  Or we shall have to take serious pause,
  And figure out if you're an angry cat,
  That may just yet make use of its claws!

# Bed Hog

You hog the bed,
    You steal the covers,
    Then we pillow fight
    Like star-crossed lovers.

You push me from you
    When you feel hot,
    Then cling, limpet-like,
    When you are not.

Our bed is your bed,
    But for one single spot:
    The spot that is wet,
    To me, you allot.

# Ass Hand

It's a subtle payback:
        You sidle up to me,
        Flirtatious, laidback;
        Running your fingers
        Across my shoulders,
        My neck, my cheeks.
        And, as you kiss me,
        Neither of us speaks.

Then, there's a smell:
        It corrodes the very air,
        Like VX or sarin gas,
        A cesspit in lowest Hell,
        Or an itinerant's ass!

I feel sluggish, lazy,
        And my vision is hazy,
        As you teasingly trail
        The polluted fingertips
        Of your soiled ass hand
        Underneath my nose,
        And between my lips.

# Mid-Sex

You start crying, mid-sex,
    Forcing me to connect
    By saying I make you happy.

I was enjoying myself:
    Now, my head's wrecked.
    Nor can I continue,
    As, half-out and half-in you –
    And no longer fully erect –
    I feel like a henpecked insect,
    Who sees you as an object,
    And I'm forced to reflect
    On why I don't feel as sappy.

# Dilemma

Far too long alone,
    And only one choice:
    The ugly bird with
    The whiney voice.

She is hideous:
    Fat; ugly as a bat;
    Has yet to evolve.
    Yet we are resolved
    That this is the night
    The dry spell is solved.

And so, we rationalise:
    She's hard on the eyes,
    But, it's either that
    Or use our own hands.
    Besides, bats are birds
    In bird-less lands.

# Barcode

In the future, they say
        Identification chips will
        Be implanted in our arms.

You are one step ahead:
        Yakuza-style tattoos;
        Engraved nipple clamps;
        Near permanent hickies;
        Slag tags and tramp stamps

You are one well-flown,
        Well-stamped passport,
        Ready to fly with any guy
        In need of a ready ass-port.

# Her Fumes

Sometime, last year,
      Her scent – it went.

On that dismal day,
      Her Eau de Parfume
      Transformed into
      Whoa! *That* perfume!
      It became Eau Dear:
      Much like the smell
      Of badly-bottled fear.
      Or even Eau de Colon:
      Sort of more ass-wiped
      Than squirted on.

It was now a repellent:
      More of a bug spray!
      Not so much alluring
      As stay-the-hell-away!
      And it fast became clear:
      She didn't want me near!

# Pandora's Box

Years on, we discover
> That every single box
> Is truly Pandora's Box.

And, when prised open
> By our rampant knife,
> We note, to our dismay
> That every single lover–
> be it girlfriend or wife–
> Is trouble, woe and strife.

Moreover, love–(obtained
> As we get our rocks off
> By unsealing that box)–
> Is then ever on the rocks.

# Cheating

It wasn't cheating:
     She came onto me,
     And I wasn't ready.
     It was an accident:
     Fleeting madness,
     Penile dementia.
     I simply forgot that
     I was going steady.
     And, when I came,
     I was filled with a
     Crushing sadness.

Still, I was away in
     Another time-zone
     When I blew my load.
     And, as it occurred
     In semi-wakefulness,
     I'll stick to the code:
     Whatever happens
     In vagueness,
     Stays in vagueness.

# R.I.P.

Deaf as a post,
    Thick as a plank,
    And horny as hell,
    She wasted years
    In her search for
    Armoured dildos,
    And even sexual
    Pecker dildos –
    As the insane do.

Then, sadly, she
    Died of fatigue by
    Going commando
    With both Squadrons
    One and Two.

# Change

Please go and find a hobby:
 I'm not one of your toys!
 I've man-things I need to do:
 After all, I'm one of the boys!
Training and watching porn;
 Poker, drinks, and clubbing;
 It has always been this way,
 So quit the endless blubbing!
If you had your fucking way,
 You and I would be at the sink,
 Chatting and bitching so much
 Our periods would be in synch!
Yet, if I simply went all female,
 You would no doubt complain,
 Declaring I was once so macho,
 And asking why I'd changed.
You'd probably rant for hours,
 Trying to turn me back into me,
 Before handing me my apron,
 And telling me to go make tea!

# Plastic

Plastic is a girl's best friend:
      Think multi-headed dildos
      Which fill up both ends.

Yet imagine her Mr Right
      With plastic vaginas or dolls:
      It would fill you with fright!

It's perverted, disgusting,
      And just terribly wrong –
      All that barbaric thrusting!

Funny, that point of view:
      It's bad if you thrust at plastic,
      But not if plastic thrusts at you!

# Helpless

Please, help me! Help me!
    I'm a frail, powerless girl!
    I'm vulnerable, defenceless,
    And ignored by the world:
    Life's kicking me senseless!

Still, there's you over there:
    You're strong enough to care,
    Protect, comfort and provide;
    Weak enough to manipulate,
    Own, and force to capitulate,
    If I occasionally open wide.

Okay, I'll fire a distress flare:
    (Look lost; sigh deeply; cry;
    Pout ; drop eyes; flick hair.)

Oh, but just before I do:
    Never ask how I survived
    In those thirty long years
    Before I latched onto you.

# Desires

She would have us:
    Give up all we love;
    Wear this, wear that;
    Prove ourselves often;
    Forever defend her;
    And love her meekly
    To the end.

We would have her:
    Take up our hobbies;
    Wear next to nothing;
    Prove herself sexually;
    Continually surrender;
    Do us thrice weekly,
    And just be a friend.

# Fluids

At sixteen, I was a boy,
     Yet I had to get into you.
     Nor did I give a damn
     What I was getting into.

We swapped mouth spit:
     You were like a new toy.
     A few tears of heartache,
     Though more tears of joy.

We shared bodily fluids:
     We spent hours petting.
     We hid in dark bedrooms:
     We didn't stop sweating.

It was twenty years later
     When I last understood:
     Despite all that I'd given,
     You now wanted my blood.

# Comparisons

Yes, she's better than you,
> In every conceivable way:
> You gave it up the first day!

She wouldn't entertain me:
> Wouldn't have me around,
> Wouldn't give any ground!

So, there's no comparison:
> You fulfil my sexual needs,
> But she can bear my seeds!

# Chiller

She was a black widow:
>A true Preying Mantis.
>A predatory man-hater
>And relationship killer.

He stayed far too long,
>Unaware of her antics,
>But, learned much later,
>He was just a hole-filler.

That girl devoured him:
>His love, life and song.

He should've eaten her,
>But never've drilled her,
>Leaving her in turmoil –
>Then just moved along.

# Hobbies

Yes, I do have hobbies:
  Amateur gynaecology,
  And propositioning.

In fact, I'll tell you what:
  I'll look you up, someday
  (Or look up you, whatever)
  And offer your ring a ring.

# Responsibility

You are primarily responsible:
>You are in charge of your womb.
>It's all down to your self-control –
>You aren't just renting out a room.

You are supposed to be selective:
>You are supposed to be choosy.
>So, don't go blaming your man
>If you've been acting the floozy.

Erect cocks have no conscience:
>Men fertilise, and they spray seed.
>So, you – or any girl – will do,
>If they need to perform the deed.

# Bridal Shower

That is the polite term:
      It's more of a slag night –
      Or a slaggle on the town.

It's no better or worse than
      Your beloved's stag night –
      Except that you suckers
      Guzzle a lot more down.

# Pure Blue Hoetry

1 – Rug and Curtains

2 – Kissing Rules

3 – She Has to Go

4 – Lie, and Take It

5 – Fuck You!

6 – Delicacy

7 – Whore

8 – Pussy Fart

9 – The Battle

10 – The Search

11 – Floppy

12 – Give it Up

13 – Primeval

14 – Phallusy

15 – Your Mother

16 – Before and After

17 – False Tits

18 – Box Sets

19 – Fantasies

20 – Cry Babies

# Rug and Curtains

You dye your hair repeatedly,
      Which makes it hard to assess
      If the rug matches the curtains
      – and so, I'm forced to guess.

Guessing is a big part of mating:
      At least, it's always been for me.
      What will that thing look like?
      What size and shape will it be?

Will its lips resemble your lips?
      Or will it look more reserved?
      Will it look war-torn and weary?
      Or will it look well-preserved?

The hair is often an indication
      Of the things I'm likely to see –
      (Messy, neatly-trimmed, tangled,
      Permed, downy-soft, spangled)
      – when I finally lay on your rug
      And you open the curtains for me.

# Kissing Rules

Your tongue is never a tentacle,
    Unless you're using it to rim.
    Nor are your lips a vacuum,
    Unless draining my 'lower him'.

You're not conducting a search
    Of my most functional cavity;
    And your lips aren't suction cups
    For docking your head to me.

You're not spraying the flowers;
    You're not breaking into song.
    Just kiss me as if you miss me,
    And you really can't go wrong.

# She Has To Go

Hey you, in the mirror –
      I told you so: She has to go!
      Lying there beside you,
      Refusing to ride you
      Because she wanted more:
      'Is this love? Is it real?
      It's just that, y'know,
      I'm beginning to… feel!'

Oh, you definitely knew!
      But you pretended to care,
      Because that tight furry pie
      Caught your lustful eye.
      And so, then and there,
      You said: 'I know, yeah,
      Because I feel that way, too!'
      Before kissing her tightly,
      And thinking: Y'know what,
      I'll even prove it to you, now,
      By pushing me into you!

# Lie, and Take It

Think of king and country:
      That is your marital duty.
      And be grateful I still care:
      You're no raving beauty.

I promise I won't be long:
      I wanked before I came in.
      Now, in my imagination,
      I'm shagging someone thin.

But you can do the same:
      You need only use your mind
      To imagine I'd dare face you,
      As I fuck you from behind.

# Fuck You!

We used to fuck –
>But then it stopped.
>The fucking stopped:
>It fucking stopped!

You fucked me over –
>That fucking sucked –
>Aware I'd take anything
>But not being fucked!
>Well, fuck you!

And now, ironically,
>That's what I need to do!
>I need to fucking fuck you
>(Not to just fuck you over,
>But to fuck you real hard,
>Or butt-fuck you real hard.)

And to keep fucking you,
>Over and over and over,
>Until you're so over-fucked
>And I'm totally fucked off
>Fucking fucking you,
>That I'm fucking over you.
>Then, fuck you!

# Delicacy

Would you eat caviar
     From a value jar?

No, I doubt it.
        So, don't come onto me
        On laundry day
        Wearing granny pants,
        Then go at the girly rants
        When I say, 'Not today!'

Don't make me shout it:
        The sweetest meat
        Should never be wrapped
        In an ass-stained sheet!

# Whore

You didn't read that right:
    It said whore in the bedroom,
    Not in the kitchen or parlour –
    Unless it's role-play night.

You're a lady in the bedroom:
    That's no fucking good to me!
    'Oh, shall I turn around now?'
    – and this said so unexcitedly.

Well, yes, I want you to do so,
    You dense little fucking whore!
    But, much like a Dickensian waif,
    I want you to beg me for more!

Then tell me about your sister –
    The time you committed *that* sin;
    And tell me how you kissed her,
    Before your mother joined in.

# Pussy Fart

If all you can dwell on
     Is your broken heart,
     Remember her loudest
     Pussy fart.

That's who she really is:
     You did right to cut ties.

She's just vibrating,
     Unintelligible flesh,
     All wrapped around
     The one true prize.

# That Battle

In that eternal battle –
    The Battle of the Sexes
    – no war is as tough as
    The Battle of the Exes.

That is the ultimate war:
    No more love juice is spilt
    – now, it's blood and gore!
    And love's fairest oaths
    Are replaced by curses,
    Foul pledges and hexes.

No! No battle is as severe,
    And no victory as rough,
    As that boldly attained from
    The ex-lover who vexes.

# The Search

Your little Black Box
    Was harder to find
    Than Batman's cave.

But when I found it,
    I sent in a canary:

And, to my relief,
    Three days later,
    It poked out a wing
    And gave me a wave.

# Floppy

No, it hasn't happened before:
    But, honestly, I wasn't stressed,
    And I *was* actually in the mood.

You just weren't at your best:
    It was the whingey-whiney face,
    And couldn't-care-less attitude.

So, I thought of somebody else
    – pretty much as I always do –
    As you were far too stroppy.

Yet, each time I opened my eyes,
    You looked like a real hard-on,
    And so my dick stayed floppy.

# Give It Up

The best part about it is,
    You actually want to,
    But are lost in dilemma:
    Will he think me a slut?

And yet, quite ironically,
    Of your three major gaps,
    The big one in your head
    Is the one that we'd rather
    You mainly kept shut!

# Primeval

Please, try to understand:
    When you bent down –
    Ass spread, baboon-like –
    Right there in front of me,
    I was hardly accountable.

You'd become available!
    You'd become mountable!
    And I – this lowly primate
    In a vastly-aroused state –
    Saw you as quite nailable!

True, we were in a chapel,
    Which invoked a little fury:
    Once, with the parishioners;
    And once more with the jury.

# Phallusy

Every wanton little cock-smith
    Has heard the giant cock myth.
    Yet nine inches –(if thinner,
    and making you feel a sinner)–
    Prods you right in the dinner.

But six inches, though fatter,
    Touches each part that matters,
    Never has trouble staying stiff,
    Provides the same baby batter,
    And is, by all accounts, a winner.

# Your Mother

What if you end up like that –
    With bingo wings and jowls?
    Forever bringing up the past,
    Wearing muumuus and cowls.

Calling everyone a bastard,
    Saying everything's changed.
    She's clearly off her meds –
    I'd even go as far as deranged!

What if you end up like that?
    Most of the time, you're a fox:
    (Mainly when I go to fuck you,
    But other times, maybe not!)

You have her hunch and lisp,
    And her cock-sucking mouth:
    I adore those, but you are gone
    The moment your tits go south!

# Before and After

About one minute beforehand:
>'Okay, legs open nice and wide:
>Now, one or two fingers inside.
>Oh, babe, I will ride you hoarse!
>I'll ride you like a rocking horse!'

About one minute afterwards:
>"Ugh! It's like a splattered crab!
>Shit! Pull your panties back on!
>It's now a badly-packed kebab,
>Filled with Abdul's special sauce!'

# False Tits

I understand:
>
> Yours were small;
>
> And cleavage is,
>
> In fact, leverage.

So, you wanted
>
> More pertness,
>
> More squeeze,
>
> And more alley.

But I'm not sure:
>
> Now, when I try
>
> To tit-wank you,
>
> It's like I'm flying
>
> A Lancaster Bomber
>
> Into Silicone Valley.

# Box Set

I've had you
  And your sister.
  But I haven't had
  Your mother yet.

One more pussy,
  That's all I need:
  Then, I'll have had
  The entire box-set.

# Fantasies

Jesus, will you stop wriggling!
>Stop talking, gurning, blinking,
>And no inappropriate giggling.

Can't you tell that I'm thinking
>Of the pretty blonde from work,
>With the big tits, the wide eyes,
>The small waist and thin thighs.

Fucking you is difficult enough
>Without you getting involved.

Here, let me turn you around
>And ram your face into a pillow:
>There we go – problem solved!

# Cry Baby

You're a regular
    Complaints department,
    And you're never, ever
    Fucking happy!

You should suck
    Dummies instead of dicks,
    And replace your lingerie,
    With a nappy!

# Deep Blue Hoetry

1 – Menstrosity

2 – Childbirth

3 – Haemo gobbler

4 – Threesome

5 – Shaving

6 – Behind

7 – Wide

8 – Nine Volts

9 – Hand Job

10 – Swinger

11 – Why I Cheated

12 – Sweats

13 – Starfish

14 – No More BJs

15 – Lezby Friends

16 – Down There

# Menstrosity

The painters are here again:
    You've started dropping clots.
    Your eyes are raw from crying,
    Your face is back out in spots.

Time to act like a crazy bitch:
    Weep, eat chocolate, cuddle;
    Curse at me like a rabid witch;
    Then do the blanket huddle.

Sit, mysterious as a sphinx:
    Suddenly turn into Mrs Hyde.
    Come at me like a wild lynx,
    Go into the bedroom and hide.

Emerge pale-faced, apologise:
    Stare at me with a teary gaze.
    Admit that you're a menstrosity,
    But lie that it's a monthly phase.

# Childbirth

Childbirth, you say?
    I've had tougher shits!

And why don't you try
    Ambidextrous wanking,
    Being kicked in the nuts,
    Catching it in a zipper,
    Facial shaving cuts,
    Or even licking one that
    Smells like a sour kipper?

# Haemo Gobbler

You are my
      Haemo gobbler:
      You, who,
      When I throw
      A wobbler
      (Driven insane,
      As I am by my
      Hairy brain)
      Convince me to
      Refrain
      From going
Captain Nemo
      And piloting my
      Hairy Nautilus
      Into your
      Mari-anus Trench
      During your
Monthly Haemo,
      By suggesting,
      Instead, that you
      Gobble me like a
      Starving wench.

# Threesome

There is only one type of threesome:
    Additional dicks are never included.
    Two lucky ladies to one happy guy:
    The other way, you must be deluded!

Ladies are built to kiss and caress;
    So, as a sex, are always more caring.
    Thusly, it's only the smallest of steps
    To being flap-mates and cock-sharing.

So, to men, this is really quite normal:
    But two dicks in you – you can't boast.
    Nor can two guys comparing cock size
    To some cum-guzzler in a spit roast!

# Shaving

The French look is over:
    No more straggly pubes.
    It's bush-whacking time:
    (Too much? Bad as moobs!)
Just a thin strip on the bits,
    But no hair under the arm.
    None on the nipples or tits –
    (Makes us recoil in alarm)
Moreover, watch the stubble:
    The wrinkly flesh and scabs
    Looks like hygiene trouble –
    As if you didn't get your jabs!
Same for the old butt crack:
    We hate a hairy backstairs!
    Keep it off, or trimmed back:
    No wild or extra-long hairs!
Still, we don't mind vajazzled,
    But not with too much bling:
    We don't want to be dazzled,
    Or lose a ring in your ring!

# Behind

If I manipulate
    Your behind
    From behind,
    Your behind –
    And its piles –
    Seemingly
    Grant me
    Toothy smiles.

And, if I paint
    The letter 'W'
    On each cheek,
    I can force
    Your cute ass
    To say 'Wow!'
    With it having
    To speak.

# Wide

Yes, I was inside:
    Just too far inside.
    Felt nothing but air:
    No flaps, no hair.

You are cave deep:
    I swear I heard seagulls.
    You may want to try
    A few million Kegels.

So, I took precautions:
    Tied a plank to my back,
    Just in case I fell into
    Your over-wide crack.

You should rent space –
    Or maybe 'go black'.
    Thing is, with no chute,
    I aint going back!

# Nine Volts

It tasted rather like
    A nine-volt battery,
    But not as pleasant.

You were game,
    But it was gamier:
    In fact, it was game
    As a poorly hung
    Pheasant.

# Hand Job

A slow, steady tug on the knob:
       Firm grip, but never strangle.
       We want increased circulation,
       And not that shrunken dangle.
       And just one hand per hand-job:
       You aren't plunging a sink.
       But if you want to use the other,
       Play carefully around the stink.

Yes, one hand, one hand only –
       And don't go chicken-plucker,
       Or stare at it through slitty eyes,
       As if you hate the little fucker!
       And, as you build momentum,
       Squeeze gently upon the sack.
       Now, start the whine-and-pine:
       Ah, there's no going back!

Now, it's time for teasing oral –
       But don't you fucking chew it!
       And only when you've blown it
       Can you say you never blew it!

# Swinger

You know you've got
>A prospective swinger,
>When she emerges
>From an unflushed
>Crapper after taking
>A nasty bowl-clinger
>(A King Kong's finger;
>A genuine tear-bringer;
>And a real humdinger,
>That is, coincidentally,
>A dead ringer for that
>Girly-voiced dead singer.)

Then, she smiles – and,
>Like that ass-stinger –
>She is totally unflushed
>And unafraid to linger.

# Why I Cheated

Basically, she loved the cock:
      She would use it as a pacifier.
      Never spoke until spoken to;
      Third date, let me ass-ify her.

Asked about me, constantly;
      Never told me her troubles.
      Didn't swallow straight away;
      Impressed me blowing bubbles.

Loved me being strong and silent.
      (I couldn't be bothered speaking)
      Offered to get herself sorted when
      She noticed the condom leaking.

She knew I didn't even like her,
      Yet she didn't dare act defeated;
      And knew I was engaged to you;
      But, unlike you, didn't feel cheated.

# Sweats

Yes, of course I love you!
    (Did you take your pill?)
    Yes, I'll stand by you!
    (Why? Are you…ill?)
    Are you really all right?
    (I'm getting a sharp chill)
    You just look so uptight…
    (Why is this all so uphill?)

No, no – I won't be mad…
    (Now, I've had my fill)
    But, *how* did you forget?
    (I so, so, *so* want to kill!)
    Yes, I *said* I'll support you!
    (Bitch, start writing a will!)

# Starfish

You're like a rubber doll:
> You don't even participate.
> Laying there like a starfish –
> Or a snare with furry bait.

Not even a gasp of delight:
> Just a whispered *oh, oh, oh!*
> For the first time in my life,
> I'd've preferred No! No! NO!

I could've got a Flesh-Light,
> Wanked with a numb hand,
> Fucked a hole in a warm pie,
> Paid for a 'one-night-stand'.

I mean, I was pumping hard:
> I was rattling the entire bed.
> But it was as if a bear was near,
> And you were playing dead!

# No More BJs

Two years in, and it stopped:
　　Once your favourite hobby,
　　You stopped sucking dick –
　　No more dining in the lobby!

I mean, I went down on you –
　　I even went *around* on you!
　　But, one day, you just ceased
　　Chugging upon the beast.

So, from now on – missionary!
　　I aint going near Old Hairy!
　　Oh, I'll fuck you now and then,
　　But, as for cunny, take a hike!

Until you start eating again,
　　I'm going on hunger strike!

# Lezby Friends

Oh, we can turn her:
    We know we can!
    That bean-flicking
    Rug-muncher
    Just needs a real man.

But, easy does it –
    Half-and-half to begin.
    First, we'll dine on her;
    Then, we'll fuck her.
    Yay! She's on solids –
    At last, one of skin!

It just takes a real man:
    And we'll step up:
    Give it to her, oh yeah,
    Hard as we fucking can!
    We'll get her hooked –
    It'll just take one lick:
    Once that veggie has us,
    She'll eat nothing but dick!

# Down there

Down there – how do I say it?
    There's way too much foliage:
    It would need to be trimmer.

It must have its own ecosystem,
    Maybe needs a park ranger,
    Or perhaps just a strimmer.

There may be soldiers in there,
    Who are sitting out some war,
    Idly awaiting a leaflet drop.

But I'm afraid to go in there,
    Just in case I get trench foot,
    Or – even worse – jungle rot!

www.ingramcontent.com/pod-product-compliance
Lightning Source LLC
Chambersburg PA
CBHW020515030426
42337CB00011B/398